CW01656723

1 SAMUEL

THE COMING KING

10 Publishing
a division of 10 of those.com

First published in Great Britain in 2018

British Library Cataloguing in Publication Data
A record for this book is available from the British Library

ISBN: 978-1-911272-68-7
Designed by Diane Warnes
Printed in the UK

10Publishing, a division of 10ofthose.com
Unit C, Tomlinson Road, Leyland, PR25 2DY, England
Email: info@10ofthose.com
Website: www.10ofthose.com

Andy Mason

31 UNDATED DEVOTIONS
THROUGH THE BOOK OF 1 SAMUEL

Done.

DAY 1 **READ** 1 Samuel 1:1–28

There have always been seasons when the people of God have seemed to be on their last legs – and have needed significant spiritual revival to keep going. 1 Samuel 1 takes place at such a time in Israel. This is a time of spiritual decay. Even worse, there don't seem to be any good spiritual leaders who are able to bring about change. There's no king (Judg. 21:25) to rally the people, and the priests aren't living as godly role models (1 Sam. 2:12).

However, despite this pervasive negative spiritual atmosphere, God is still at work to bring change. The change doesn't come, though, through the spiritual hierarchy of Eli the priest and his family, but through the simple and desperate prayer of a bullied and barren woman, Hannah. This is God's surprise in the story. Her 'bitterness of soul' (v. 10) in childlessness leads her not to unbelief but to prayer (v. 11). For Hannah, anxiety and disappointment don't serve as barriers to prayer but, on the contrary, they become her spiritual rocket fuel!

This prayer has a greater significance, though. It will, remarkably, be the means by which God raises up a new leader, Samuel (v. 20), who will bring the much-needed spiritual change to Israel. We should be encouraged by this to see our prayers in light of God's big global plans and purposes. Forgotten, harassed and unimportant people on their knees in prayer are more powerful than princes and priests.

As she promised (v. 11), Hannah, with supreme faith, dedicates the precious answer to her prayer, her only son, to the Lord (vv. 24–28). She teaches us that we really can dare to give over the most valuable things in our lives to the Lord, even when they've been given to us miraculously! We have even better reasons to do so than Hannah because we've experienced our God giving up and dedicating his own precious Son for us. Hannah gave her son up to temple service, but the Father gave up his Son to the cross for our sake.

REFLECTION

1. Why is prayer so powerful?

2. Is there anything in your life that you're refusing to give away to the Lord for his use? How does the Father's offering up of his Son change your heart on this?

Done.

DAY 2

READ 1 Samuel 2:1–10

Things don't always go as you expect. Whether it's national elections, or the mundane details of our lives, we're constantly caught off guard and humbled by the events of life. 1 Samuel comes back to this idea a lot, as we see again and again that fortunes are reversed by the Lord's plans. The powerful lose their power. The arrogant are exposed. The underdog becomes top dog. The weak overcome the strong. 1 Samuel is full of the rise of the humble and the fall of the proud, all guided by the sovereign hand of a God who does the unexpected.

Hannah's prayer of praise in these verses is a reminder and insight into how fortunes are reversed. She knows that it is only through the Lord that her own barrenness had been overcome (v. 1). She had been harassed and bullied, but has now been raised up by the Lord through the birth of Samuel (v. 5). This is our wonderful God. As Hannah says in verse 2, 'there is no-one besides you'. Here we have solid ground in the middle of shifting fortunes: 'there is no Rock like our God'.

Even more striking, Hannah's mini experience of salvation becomes, in the prayer, a picture of a much bigger salvation for God's people. The birth of Samuel will indeed bring big changes. Whole armies will be overcome (v. 4) and hungry multitudes will be fed (v. 5). A new justice will come as rich oppressors lose their power and the oppressed are saved (vv. 6–8, 10). In other words, Hannah's answered prayer isn't just for her, but for the people. The prayer is even for us, because it looks forward to the birth of a greater baby who will reverse the fortunes of many (Luke 1:46–55). A strong and exalted king is coming (v. 10) to save the people.

REFLECTION

1. Why do you think the Lord has a habit of reversing the fortunes of the proud and the weak? What's his purpose in that?

2. What in this prayer encourages you to trust the Lord more when you pray to him?

Done.

DAY 3

READ 1 Samuel 2:11–36

The religious and spiritual labels that spiritual leaders use can be very misleading. Whether it's 'Reverend', 'Pastor' or 'Bishop', labels don't, in and of themselves, tell you about the faith or righteousness of those leaders.

However, no-one could be deceived about the spiritual leaders in this chapter. Here we find a description of the elite spiritual leadership in Israel, who ministered at the well-known spiritual centre of Shiloh. First of all, we meet the 'sons of Eli', who prove to be greedy hypocrites, stealing food from the Lord's sacrifices (vv. 13–16) and sleeping around with their co-workers (v. 22). Their behaviour was a scandal even to the common people (vv. 16, 23). As a result, they stood condemned before the Lord (vv. 17, 25, 34). The Lord doesn't look at labels, but the reality of our lives.

Then we meet, Eli, their father. He knew their behaviour was a scandal, and knew that they were on a collision course with the Lord (vv. 23–25). Yet, Eli hadn't dismissed his sons, and his action to stop them proved to be weak and ineffective. The corruption of these leaders, then, isn't just about blatant immorality, but also about the failure of others to discipline and properly correct the immorality (v. 29; 3:13). It's not just the sons who are at fault, but also Eli, who doesn't deal with their behaviour (see the prophecy of coming judgment in verses 27–36). Failure on the part of spiritual leaders to deal with blatant sin makes them, in part, guilty for that sin.

Amidst the evil, though, the Lord is at work (see verses 18–19, 26). He's raising Samuel up as a true priest and deliverer for the people (v. 35). There are fierce warnings and judgments in this chapter, but God's grace is also at work to revive his messed-up people. Where sin had increased, grace increased all the more.

REFLECTION

1. Why does spiritual leadership become corrupt? What can we do to stop it?

2. How can we be certain that God's people will never be overwhelmed by the sins of any leaders?

DAY 4

READ 1 Samuel 3:1 – 4:1

We've already seen the spiritual mess of God's people in these opening chapters of 1 Samuel. There's a need for revival and good spiritual leadership to resolve the mess. But, above all, what God's people really need is to recover the word of the Lord. In verse 1 we read that 'the word of the LORD was rare' at the time. It wasn't quite a famine of the word (cf. Amos 8:11), but it was a lack of the word. The people were getting by with the bare minimum of spiritual sustenance. The good news now, though, is that the word is about to come afresh.

The surprise in this story, though, is the one to whom the word comes. It isn't the experienced priest, Eli, who receives the word, but the boy apprentice, Samuel. Again, we see God's way of reversing fortunes. Eli has high status, but is an unfaithful priest. He is now brought down, while Samuel, inexperienced and with no special lineage, is raised up. God our Father is an impartial Judge (1 Pet. 1:17) and no respecter of human privilege or background. Samuel has become God's prophet bringing God's word (v. 8). The word is spoken through Samuel first to Eli (vv. 15–18), and then to the people (3:20 – 4:1). A new era has dawned as God's word becomes available again.

We can be thankful today that we don't have to wait for a prophet to come to bring us God's word, but we have the incredible privilege of having God's complete written word completely available to us. Further, we don't, through the Bible, have access to only one great prophet, but we can listen to many prophets and apostles. In fact, we have access to the Son of God himself, who has brought us God's final word (Heb. 1:1–2). Let's value that word today!

REFLECTION

1. What's so bad about not having access to God's word? What happens as a result?

2. How can you take advantage of the privileged access to God's word that you have today?

DAY 5

READ 1 Samuel 4:1–22

The Bible's message is fundamentally good news, but there's no hiding the fact that this passage, from start to finish, is full of shocking bad news. This is one very dark day in the history of God's people, as the earlier prophecy of judgment given to Eli is now fulfilled (2:27–34).

The first shock is national (vv. 1–11): Israel experiences a shocking defeat at the hands of the Philistines. In desperate straits, they had turned to the power of the ark of God to save them, but God will not be used as a lucky charm. They receive precious little help from the ark as God gives them over to judgment for their sins. The Philistines overwhelm them (v. 10) and they're utterly humiliated as the ark, the throne of God, is itself captured (v. 11).

The second shock is personal (vv. 12–18): Eli receives a terrible emotional blow as he hears of the death of his two sons, Hophni and Phinehas, in battle (vv. 16–17). The tragedy continues as Eli, upon also hearing of the loss of the ark, literally falls over with shock and breaks his neck. The corrupt spiritual leaders of Israel are finally wiped out in judgment.

The last shock has to do with the spiritual legacy of this terrible day (vv. 19–22). The wife of Phinehas sadly dies in child birth. Though her son survives, he becomes the spiritual epitaph for this day: as Phineas's wife is dying, she names him 'Ichabod', meaning 'no glory'. In other words, God's powerful glory and presence, symbolised by the ark of God, has now left his people. The judgment is complete.

The bad news in this story is a warning for us. God isn't fooled by spirituality, church activity or the use of religious rituals. Without true faith and repentance in our lives, we're walking on thin ice. False religion, whatever its position and influence, is under judgment. Let's not follow others into that judgment.

REFLECTION

1. Why do we need to hear the shocking bad news in this story?

2. What kind of 'arks' might we trust in today to get us out of difficult situations? Where will that lead us?

Done

DAY 6

READ 1 Samuel 5:1–12

When we see God's church weakened and under discipline, it's easy to think that our enemies have won – and even that the Lord has lost control. This passage teaches us, though, that the appearance of defeat can be deceptive.

In chapter 4 we read about Israel's shocking defeat at the hands of God's enemies, the Philistines, which led to the capture of the ark of God. The chapter ended with the depressing conclusion that the glory of God had now left Israel. The Philistines, flush with victory and cocky in their superiority, then set up the captured ark in the temple of their god Dagon as a nationalistic war trophy. It seemed like Israel's God had obviously been defeated.

The story shows us, though, that the defeat of God's people is never the defeat of their God. He remains utterly sovereign and holy. Accordingly, the placement of the ark, the symbol of God's presence, in Dagon's temple proves to be a fatal error for the Philistines. The initial warning comes as Dagon, in his own temple, ends up mysteriously prostrating himself before the Lord in total subjection (vv. 3–4). Israel's God proves to be a devastating holy presence, who, quite literally, blows Dagon apart (v. 4). The Philistines quickly notice that a curse has come upon them – the Lord's holy presence has 'brought devastation upon them' (v. 6). Worried, they try to remove the ark to another city, but disaster, death and mayhem result as they experience the difficulty of living with a holy God.

The ups and downs of God's church never reflect ups and downs in our God's sovereignty and power. Some may talk about Christianity dying out in our society, but the Bible draws a different conclusion. The Lord rules over every enemy and every idol at every moment – even when they seem, on the surface, to be winning. No-one can domesticate, dominate or defeat the holy God of the Bible.

REFLECTION

1. Why shouldn't the weakening, or seeming defeats, of God's church undermine our faith?

2. How do we know that our God has not been defeated? From the passage, why is it foolish for people to treat God as 'dead' or unimportant?

DONE.

DAY 7

READ 1 Samuel 6:1 – 7:1

In these chapters of 1 Samuel we're learning just how holy the God of Israel is: 'Who can stand in the presence of the LORD, this holy God?' (6:20). The Philistines are learning this to their cost. Their defeat of Israel in chapter 5 proved to be a very hollow victory, as God's holy ark brought devastating judgment upon them.

In verses 3–12 we see the Philistines' sad confusion as they try to deal with a holy God. They recognise that they're under judgment in some way (v. 3) and that God is holding them to account (v. 6), but they don't know how their guilt should be dealt with (v. 4). The best they can do is to make an offering (v. 4) – one that God clearly doesn't want with a vague hope that it might all work out in the end (v. 5). Human religion, to the extent that it knows God as holy, always tries to manage his holiness with its own efforts and offerings. Such religion can only see God as a Judge to be escaped from because it doesn't know how to come before him. Reading this, we can't help but see what a privilege it is to have had the gospel preached and explained to us!

However, God's holiness isn't just a problem for the pagan Philistines. In verses 6:13 – 7:1 we see presumption amongst those who belong to God. Initially, the return of the ark brings an exciting revival as God's people in Beth Shemesh offer him right worship. Notice, ironically, how it's the accompanying cart and cattle, not the offered tumours and rats, that provide the right way of coming before a holy God. Yet, the people's worship proves fatal as they too become casual with the holy ark in verse 19. This time it's Israelites, not Philistines, who are struck down.

So, as we come to our holy God, let's make sure that we're walking by faith in Christ's death, and not with presumption. And, as we rejoice in having free access through Jesus, let's respect and remember the awesome holiness of the God we worship.

REFLECTION

1. Why can't human religion make us fit to come before our holy God? we are sinners.

2. What might tempt us to presumption as we come before our holy God?

Pride.

DAY 8

READ 1 Samuel 7:2–17

God's people need spiritual leadership. The ongoing problem in Israel, right from the beginning of 1 Samuel, was the absence of any decent spiritual leadership. The people's corruption had first started with the corruption of their leaders. Ultimately, that led to devastating defeat at the hands of the Philistines, yet, in the middle of it all, the Lord was at work. He was raising up a new judge and spiritual leader, Samuel (2:35), who would lead the people back to God. In this chapter we see that plan fulfilled.

Samuel is vital here in the people's spiritual revival, as well as leading them to victory over the Philistines. He leads them by fearlessly preaching repentance (v. 3), by praying for them in their mess (vv. 5, 9) and by faithfully pastoring them over the long haul (vv. 16–17). In all of this he's dependent on God, knowing that it's not his human skill that delivers Israel, but the Lord's (v. 12). This is what we need our spiritual leaders to be doing for us.

Yet, also notice the importance of the people's responsiveness to right spiritual leadership. Crucially, they're willing to be led. They seek the Lord (v. 2), repent at Samuel's preaching (v. 4), confess their sin (v. 6) and seek Samuel's help (v. 8). No spiritual leader can lead people who don't want to be led. It's worth asking ourselves today whether we're willing to be led by those leaders the Lord has put over us?

Of course, the ultimate leader over the church isn't a man, but the Lord Jesus. Samuel's sacrifice (v. 9) and altar-building (v. 17) aren't patterns for today's spiritual leaders, but point us to the work of Christ himself. Jesus is the one who brings us complete victory (cf. vv. 13–14) over our biggest enemies – sin, the world and the devil. If Israel could rest secure in Samuel's leadership, how much more can we rest *absolutely* secure in the protection of Jesus, the ultimate Judge.

REFLECTION

1. What is your relationship like with your spiritual leaders? Will you let them lead you?

2. What difference does it make if you're secure with your ultimate Judge today?

Whereas chapter 7 celebrates the importance of leadership, chapter 8 warns us of the danger of leadership. We should read these chapters together.

The good news of vibrant spiritual leadership in chapter 7 is short-lived. Tragically, we see that Samuel's own family (vv. 1–3) is starting to echo all the spiritual problems of Eli's family in 2:12. We're reminded not to put our faith in human leaders, however godly they are, as they're tainted with the same sin problems as we are. That said, it's also a reminder for every leader to make the spiritual needs of their own family an overwhelming priority in their lives.

The response of the people, however, only compounds the problems of leadership in Israel. Rather than turning once again to the Lord for help and guidance, they put their hope in a king like the nations around them (v. 5). They plan a spiritual coup whereby the King of kings is replaced with a puny, powerless man. Understandably, the Lord takes this rejection very personally (vv. 7–9).

It should be said, though, that it wasn't, in and of itself, wrong for Israel to have a king. Deuteronomy 17:14–20 permitted kings in Israel and outlined how godly kingship should look. The problem here was, rather, to do with the kind of king Israel was looking for, namely, a god-like saviour who would deal with all their problems. The hope for a god-like human leader has been a dangerous thing throughout the history of the world, with dictators both inside and outside the church bringing destruction in their wake. The destructiveness of Israel's hoped-for king is foretold in verses 11–18, yet, ironically, the people remain determined to have a king.

We should never give our hearts to any celebrity leader, pastor, speaker or writer – and certainly not to any political leader or guru. Our hearts belong to the Lord alone. We have one King, and his name is Jesus. Let's rejoice in him, and not try to replace him with some puny human substitute.

REFLECTION

1. Why are we so drawn to setting up human leaders?

2. What can Jesus do that no human leader ever can?

DAY 10

READ 1 Samuel 9:1–24

There are no coincidences in God's world. Every event and detail is purposed and planned by an almighty God. We see that absolute control in this chapter. The story might, at first, seem strange, but it's actually the outworking of God's secret purpose for Israel and Saul. Previously in chapter 8, the people of Israel had displeased the Lord by asking for a king. At the end of chapter 8, the Lord's tone is dismissive as he says to Samuel, 'give them a king' (8:22). It may therefore look as if the Lord has withdrawn from his people, but this story shows us that he is still at work as he makes Saul king over his people (see v. 16).

Every insignificant detail and event here is used in the Lord's purpose to get Saul to meet up with Samuel. The loss of the donkeys (vv. 3–5) seems like a strange and irrelevant event. However, it is the means by which Saul is led out of his local community to Samuel. Saul is ready to go home, but his servant suggests that they consult with a nameless 'man of God' (v. 6). Coming to the town where he is rumoured to be, they bump into some girls and ask where the man of God is (v. 11). Amazingly, they learn he had come to the town on the same day as Saul (v. 12). Next, they bump into Samuel himself (v. 14), who had already been told by the Lord that he would lead Saul to the prophet (v. 16). In other words, the Lord is in control of every one of Saul's steps here, and he uses missing donkeys, servants, journey timings, teenage girls and direct revelation to bring about his purpose for his king and his people.

There are no coincidences in our life. This doesn't mean we always know what is happening, nor does it mean that we have to work out why certain things have happened. But we're simply given the assurance that the Lord is working out his purpose amidst all the insignificant details of our life, whether it involves donkeys or not!

REFLECTION

1. What difference does it make knowing that you're not given over to fate or luck, but to the Lord's purpose?

2. As you look back over your life so far, can you see any purposes of God that have been worked out?

DAY 11

READ 1 Samuel 9:25 – 10:27

We've already seen in chapter 9 how the Lord, behind the scenes, has been working out his plan to make Saul king. Finally, Saul has met God's prophet, Samuel, and he's about to become the very first (human) king of Israel. This chapter is full, though, of big contrasts.

On the one hand, we see that Saul is the *Lord's king*. In 9:1–8 every step and personal encounter with this new king is purposefully guided by the Lord, as Saul receives God's word directly through Samuel. In verses 9–11 he's dramatically filled with God's Spirit, and is given a changed heart and powerful prophetic gifts. Finally, in verse 24 Saul is confirmed as the Lord's chosen king. It's clear that Saul hasn't appointed himself, but has been called out by God.

On the other hand, we see a lot of *uncertainty* with this new king. Saul himself seems cowardly and fickle about his new role (vv. 15–16, 21–23). Rather surprisingly, though the Lord has orchestrated all the events, his word to Israel in verses 18–19 is very scathing: Israel will get their new king, but they have rejected the very God who has saved them in the past. Finally, even some Israelites are left uncertain about Saul being their king (v. 27). So, though verse 24 tells us that Saul is the Lord's chosen king, we're also left wondering if he really is the king that the Lord wants. This chapter gives us a very uncertain picture of Saul.

We'll see this double-sided view of Saul work itself out in the chapters that follow. He is, it seems, the Lord's king, but, ultimately, he doesn't live up to that role. Thankfully, we're not in that situation today, as we have a better king with whom there's no uncertainty. Our King isn't unclear about his role, nor is he hiding amongst the baggage. On the contrary, he's risen from the dead, filled with the Spirit and rules with uncontested power.

REFLECTION

Look at Matthew 3:11–17.

1. In what way is Jesus' relationship with the Spirit greater than Saul's?

2. In what way is the Father's affirmation of Jesus greater than Saul's?

DAY 12

READ 1 Samuel 11:1–15

We have a duty of care to our brothers and sisters in Christ, no matter who they are or where they're based. Our Father has made us one another's keepers, and we're to fulfil Christ's law by carrying one another's burdens (Gal 6:2). This passage is about a dereliction of that duty to care.

In verse one an Israelite community, Jabesh Gilead, is besieged and threatened by a foreign warlord, Nahash. He threatens to humiliate and blind the right eye of the whole population of the city (vv. 2–3). Understandably, the alarm is sent out by the city as they ask for help from the rest of Israel. The response is weak, but Saul, previously the nervous and unassured king, now steps up to the mark. Notice the connection between being filled with the Spirit of God and anger (v. 6). There is obviously a kind of righteous anger that is very Spirit-driven. Saul, angry not only at Nahash, but also at the passivity of the people of Israel, issues a very strong threat to Israel (v. 7). The response is immediate, and Nahash and his bandits are wiped out.

Of course, it's much better to be motivated by love and compassion, but the reality of sin amongst even God's people is such that, at times, we'll only be motivated by threats and discipline. There are threats in Scripture (for example, in Gal. 5:19–21) and we would be wise to listen to them. Even better, let's be responsive to the needs of believers around us, particularly persecuted believers, without having to be threatened.

This is a day of success for Saul, not just in terms of military power, but also in character. With his new-found authority he refuses to take revenge on his enemies, but honours the Lord in what has happened (v. 13), and is confirmed as the Lord's king (vv. 14–15). God's kingdom is established not by might, but in righteousness. The character of the kingdom matters.

REFLECTION

1. What blinds us to the needs of other believers around us? Where do we need to be more responsive?

2. Why might success sometimes lead us to neglect character? What kind of character should we be showing in the midst of success?

DAY 13

READ 1 Samuel 12:1–25

A new kingdom has come to Israel, as Saul is confirmed as the new king at Gilgal (11:14–15). Yet, there's some uncertainty about what kind of kingdom this will be. It had started in rebellion against the Lord (8:7–8), but the good news in this chapter is that past failures and sins don't have to dominate the present. If God's people will walk faithfully in the present, then they'll experience new grace for today. So, as Samuel hands the baton onto Saul, what will this kingdom be – the kingdom of God on earth, or something more sinister (see 8:10–18)?

As he steps down, Samuel is clear that he leaves a legacy of integrity (vv. 1–5). Israel's failure isn't his fault (unlike with Eli earlier). Samuel has lived a life of honesty, fairness and right relationships, which the people can confirm. Wouldn't it be great if, when asked about the integrity of our lives, the people who know us well might be able to respond similarly?

Next, Samuel reminds the people of the Lord's grace down through time (vv. 8–11). This isn't a people who've been treated harshly by their God, but, again and again, they've experienced his mercy and provision in the midst of continual sin. Accordingly, their asking for a king hadn't just been sinful, but it had been sin against God's amazing grace. The sobering fact is that because every believer has received God's grace, every sin in a believer's life is a sin against grace.

The choice for Israel now, then, is whether or not to remain faithful and obedient in the present (vv. 14–15). If so, they'll receive new grace. Yes, they've displeased the Lord in the past (vv. 16–18), but they have the privilege of Samuel seeking the Lord on their behalf (vv. 19, 23) and the promise of the Lord's committed love (v. 22). Similarly, whatever has been happening in your life, don't be held back by your past, but 'consider what great things he has done for you' (v. 24). Come back to the Lord's grace for your present and seek to obey him today.

REFLECTION

1. How can you see God's grace at work in your life over the last few years?

2. Where might you need to confess sin in your life today? How can you make sure that you're trusting his grace for you today and moving forward in obeying the Lord?

DAY 14

READ 1 Samuel 13:1–15

It's always worth listening to advice and warning, particularly when it comes from God (see 8:7–18). We now read the reason for the warning. In chapter 11 there was a moment of great promise as King Saul defeated Nahash and rescued Israel. In chapter 12 Samuel gave a fresh warning to the people, but, above all, promised the Lord's continued love if they would obey him. Yet now, in chapter 13, we have major spiritual disaster as the new kingdom spiritually fractures - almost as soon as it gets going. Sadly, this will go on for another 42 years (v. 1).

The Philistines, Israel's great enemy, come in vast numbers to attack Israel (v. 5). The people, cowering before them, retreat (v. 6) and Saul's army is left cowering in a corner (v. 7). Saul, meanwhile, is waiting for Samuel to come (see 10:8) to offer sacrifice and prayer for the threatened kingdom. King Saul sees his kingdom falling apart, and Samuel seems to be coming late, so, in desperation, he makes the sacrifices himself, calling upon God to intervene (v. 12). Samuel then arrives, either late or just in the nick of time, and is shocked by Saul's arrogance. Saul had no right to do this as he isn't Israel's high priest or mediator. Above all, Saul has disobeyed Samuel's (therefore God's) command (v. 13). Saul's sin was to think that performing the sacrifice was more important the obeying the word of God. We're reminded that God doesn't want our rituals, however well-intentioned, but he wants us to keep his commands. In crises, don't rely upon talismans and superstitions, or even church rituals, but follow what God has said.

Saul's disobedience, sadly for him, will lead to the removal of his kingdom and the raising up of another king (vv. 13–14). For the first time, we hear the promise of the 'man after [God's] own heart' – the hope of a truly obedient king. In 1 Samuel this will be David, but ultimately it will be Jesus Christ. Sin and failure in Saul will, in God's purpose, lead to the establishing of a greater kingdom built on a greater King.

REFLECTION

1. Are you listening to God's warnings in your life?

2. Why does God want us to obey his word rather than rely upon rituals?

3. How do we see Jesus living as the 'man after [God's] own heart'?

DAY 15

READ 1 Samuel 13:16 – 14:23

Courage is a much undervalued part of Christian character. It's not something that's mentioned lots, but it's vital for discipleship. How can we ever hope to take up our cross and follow Jesus without courage? This passage teaches us about the importance of courage. The background is Israel's helplessness and hopelessness in the face of Philistine raiding parties (13:16–22). Most of the army has deserted, and Saul and his army are essentially in hiding.

In the middle of this, we see the 'crazy', faith-filled courage of Jonathan (14:6). He reasons that the best defence is a good offence. He decides, together with his armour bearer, to mount a tiny, brazen, all-out assault on a Philistine fort. This is the definition of risk-taking. Jonathan knows, though, that numbers and strength, and even swords (13:22), don't matter to God. Wisely, Jonathan doesn't presume to know what the Lord will do (notice the 'perhaps' in 14:6), but he knows what the Lord *can* do. Amazingly, it's a massive success as the whole Philistine army is routed (v. 15).

The contrasts between Jonathan and Saul in this story are obvious. While Jonathan is racing up a cliff, Saul is sat under a pomegranate tree (v. 2). While Jonathan wields his sword, Saul has his sword tucked in its sheath. While Jonathan only has his armour bearer for reinforcements, Saul has six hundred men. While Jonathan is leading the army, Saul is sitting around. While Jonathan trusts the Lord, Saul is hanging out with Ahijah, from Eli's rejected line of priests (v. 3). When we set Jonathan up against Saul, we see that Saul's carefulness isn't godly prudence, but cowardice.

We're not called to be fools, but when did we last do something 'crazy' for Jesus? Has our carefulness become a spiritual trap? Or is our confidence in the Lord giving us courage in our discipleship? If we want to see amazing things from God, we will have to risk amazing things for God.

REFLECTION

1. How much have you thought about courage as an important part of Christian character?

2. What fuels Christian courage? What fuels sinful cowardice?

DAY 16

READ 1 Samuel 14:24–52

How should we measure someone's life? We're constantly tempted to assess the success of someone's life by their achievements, money and influence. Saul has, in many ways, gained these things:

- he's the national leader
- he's experienced great military victory (vv. 47–48)
- he's established a royal family and built a team of leaders (vv. 49–52)

This is a successful man in the eyes of the world. Yet, our passage shows us that, amidst his success, he's also a very foolish man. Worldly success and wisdom aren't the same things.

The passage is dominated by Saul's rash vow in verse 24 (vows were solemn and serious things in the ancient world). This vow forbade his troops from eating anything until they had obliterated the enemy. This was undoubtedly a foolish and reckless thing to do. Saul's vow was unnecessary, oppressive for his men and militarily stupid (vv. 29–30). Further, it caused the men, driven by extreme hunger and fatigue, to break the food laws in Leviticus 17 (vv. 31–35). Saul's unwise leadership actually undermined the spiritual integrity of Israel. All in all, it seems that this vow was driven more by his ego and need for revenge than the good of the kingdom.

The low point in it all is reached when Saul, out of a distorted mixture of pride and religiosity, almost executes his own son, Jonathan. Saul feels that the Lord isn't guiding him (vv. 37–39), and so draws lots to find out who is behind this. Jonathan had, earlier, unwittingly broken the vow (v. 27), and the lot exposes him (vv. 41–42). Saul seems intent on keeping his vow to execute the culprit (v. 44), but everyone else thinks he's being absurd (vv. 43, 45). Funnily enough, in the end, it's Saul's own men who have to save Jonathan from his own dad.

Saul's foolishness shows us that the priority in God's kingdom isn't success, but wisdom. Let's make sure we're seeking that wisdom, whatever other success the Lord might grant us in our lives.

REFLECTION

1. How can success make us act unwisely? What is true wisdom?

2. Where are you in danger of acting foolishly in your life? Where do you need wisdom today?

DAY 17

READ 1 Samuel 15:1–35

This passage shows us the spiritual disaster that comes from disregarding the Lord's instructions. It doesn't matter who we are, or what our role in the kingdom is; none of us are above God's word.

Admittedly, the word that is given to Saul is a hard one (vv. 1–3). It calls him to wipe out the Amalekites. We're obviously shocked by this, but we should remember that this was the punishment for their own war crimes (see v. 33) and treatment of God's people (v. 2). This punishment hadn't been quick but slow to come (literally hundreds of years). Saul, though, doesn't keep the Lord's command and spares King Agag as well as the best of their sheep and cattle (vv. 8–9). Superficially, he excuses this plunder as being for worship (v. 21), but in reality it was done out of wanting to please the people more than God (v. 24). Saul is both arrogant (v. 12) and ignorant (v. 20) in his disobedience to God's word.

Saul has now gone too far and the Lord rejects him, because Saul rejects the Lord's word (v. 26). The sad desperation of Saul as he realises what he had done is tragic (v. 27). He confesses his sin (vv. 24, 30), but it is too late. Samuel, the one who gives Saul God's word, never sees Saul again (v. 35).

Are we obeying God in our life? He doesn't want our superficial sacrifices, outward displays of religiosity and big words – he wants our specific obedience to his word. True worship of God is about doing what his word says, and, therefore, ignoring his word is a basic rejection of him (see vv. 22–23).

We read in verse 28 that the kingdom will be given to another, as a disobedient king could never lead God's people into obedience. Ultimately, King Jesus is the one who lived out the perfectly obedient life – on our behalf. He is now empowering us day by day for a new obedience to God's word in our lives (2 Cor. 3:18).

REFLECTION

1. What needs to happen in your life today for you to grow in obedience to God?

2. How does the Lord Jesus' obedience on your behalf encourage you today in your walk with him?

DAY 18

READ 1 Samuel 16:1–23

What kind of things do people look for when they're voting in national leaders? Charisma? Good looks? Dynamism? Good speaking abilities? Human beings can't help but be impressed by certain outward leadership abilities. The Lord, however, isn't impressed by surface competence; rather, the Lord looks at the heart (v. 7).

In this passage we're introduced, for the first time, to David, the man after God's own heart (13:14). 1 Samuel began with a corrupt priesthood, led by Eli, then it moved to Samuel, God's appointed judge. Now something similar happens: Saul, the rejected king, gives way to the Lord's chosen king, David. Saul declines in power while David is raised up to the throne. David isn't the natural choice, though – even God's prophet can't see why he should be king (vv. 6–12)! We're reminded that the Lord doesn't do things according to man's wisdom (v. 7). Of course, this is pointing us to the true king, Jesus, the man of sorrows rejected by men (Is. 53:3–4).

Though outwardly Saul is still king and David is still a shepherd, a radical change has happened. They are utterly different men before God. Saul was once a man of the Spirit (10:10), but is now afflicted only by evil spirits (v. 14). David, on the hand, is the Lord's anointed, filled with the Spirit (v. 13). Through God's remarkable sovereign control of events (see 9:1–24), David ends up in Saul's palace (vv. 15–21). Ironically, the true, unacknowledged, Spirit-filled king is the one who brings comfort to the rejected, tormented, ruling king (v. 23). We see the Lord's mercy to Saul in this, but, above all, we see the weakness of the visible ruling king versus the spiritual strength of the hidden king.

We shouldn't be fooled by appearances. Jesus, though hidden, really is reigning as the risen king. His true power and glory is obscured to the world at the moment, but it doesn't make it any less real. That should bolster our faith and teach us not to live by appearances in our day-to-day lives.

REFLECTION

1. Why are we so easily led astray by outward appearances? How is that different to God's way of doing things?

2. How do you see the 'hidden' power of the Lord Jesus at work in the world today?

DAY 19

READ 1 Samuel 17:1–54

Chapter 16 made it clear that the Lord, in contrast to us, doesn't look at the outward appearance, but at the heart. This famous story of David and Goliath is a great demonstration of that principle. Goliath seems in charge, but God has other plans.

The giant Philistine, Goliath, with his massive muscles and armed to the teeth, challenges and taunts God's people (vv. 4–10). Unfortunately, the response of Saul and his armies is cowardly and cowering (v. 11). Again, Saul fails as king. It's up to David, not Saul, to step forward as the Saviour-King of God's people here. David is a young shepherd boy (vv. 12–15), mocked by his older brothers (v. 28) and seemingly ill-equipped for battle (vv. 38–39). Outwardly, he is nothing before the towering, frightening Goliath. But, God has already secretly prepared this shepherd boy to be Israel's anointed king. He has been filled with the Spirit (16:13). He has already fought with wild animals (vv. 34–37). And, above all, he has been given faith and courage (vv. 26, 36, 45–47). David knows that the battle belongs to the Lord (vv. 37, 46). He is truly a man after God's own heart.

The surprising end of the story brings victory through weakness (vv. 48–49). It's the slingshot of David that wins, and not a sword. As a result, the Philistines suffer humiliating defeat at the hands of the armies of Israel (vv. 51–54). Israel's victory, though, hasn't come through their own strategy and weaponry, but through the courage of another. Someone else has fought and won on behalf of the people.

Isn't this story an amazing picture of the gospel? Jesus, the anointed king, came in weakness and servanthood. He too was rejected by many, even his own brothers. He too entrusted himself to the Lord and walked by faith. And in a way that no-one expected, at the cross, he defeated the giants of sin, death and the devil. We haven't won through our efforts, but we get to enjoy the victory of a great Saviour-King who has fought on our behalf.

REFLECTION

1. Why do you think God saves his people through a seemingly weak king?

2. To what extent are you resting in what Jesus has already done for you, or do you still feel that you have to achieve it all yourself?

DAY 20

READ 1 Samuel 17:55 – 18:30

The kingdom of the world has always been in conflict with the kingdom of God. In our passage this conflict is made personal in the difficult relationship between Saul, the rejected king, and David, the Lord's chosen king.

It's clear that Saul can't stand David and his success. The victory over Goliath wasn't just a one-off, but was the beginning of a new power in Israel. David's rule flourishes and increases because the Lord is with him (18:12, 14, 28). Everything he now does is successful (vv. 5, 7, 14, 15, 27, 30). He has become famous (vv. 7, 30) and is loved by the people (vv. 6, 16). Even Saul's own family adore David and pledge loyalty to him (vv. 1–4, 28).

Saul, by way of contrast, is rejected (v. 12). Though gifted, he's filled with evil (v. 10), dominated by insane jealousy of David (vv. 9, 10–11), and is fearful of David's growing influence (vv. 15, 29). Accordingly, feeling under threat, Saul secretly plots and conspires to have David killed (vv. 20–21, 25). The kingdom of the world really can't stand the kingdom of God!

Saul's hatred of David in chapter 18 is a taste of the world's hatred for King Jesus. Jesus himself tells us that we shouldn't be surprised if the world hates us, because it hated him first (John 15:18). Therefore, while we shouldn't give in to paranoia, we shouldn't be surprised if the world conspires against the church. If that does happen, we should deal with our enemies in the same way that the chosen king does. Notice how David, amazingly, doesn't revolt against Saul despite intense provocation. Rather, his attitude towards Saul remains remarkably humble and submissive (vv. 18, 23). This is a pattern for us. However the world treats us, let's return hatred with the love and humility of David, and ultimately of Jesus himself.

REFLECTION

1. Where do you see, or experience, the world's dislike of the kingdom of God?

2. How are you responding to that dislike? How does David (and the Lord Jesus) set you a pattern for your life today?

DAY 21

READ 1 Samuel 19:1–24

The Lord has raised David up as his chosen king in Israel. He has been successful in everything he has done (see 18:5, 14) and has become extremely popular (18:16). However, in God's plan, this king isn't destined to take over painlessly from Saul. Saul won't be simply wiped out to make way for David as the new king. On the contrary, the Lord's plan is for his chosen king to be a *persecuted* king. The plots against David started in chapter 18. They reach a high point in chapter 19 when Saul, having failed in previous attempts, now sends his own soldiers to kill David. The result is that David has to run for his life from Saul to Samuel (v. 18).

The remarkable thing in this chapter, though, is *how* the Lord protects David. David is the Goliath-slayer and a mighty warrior (v. 8), but the Lord saves David through weakness and vulnerability. There are four attempts on David's life here. The first attempt is only thwarted because of the intervention of Jonathan (vv. 1–7). The second attempt fails only because David manages to escape Saul's clutches while he's under the influence of an evil spirit (vv. 9–10). The third attempt fails only through the intervention and worldly wisdom of his wife (vv. 11–17). The final attempt is remarkably defeated through the sheer power of the Spirit controlling the soldiers and finally Saul himself (vv. 18–24).

In other words, it isn't David's military prowess or strategy that save him, but the Lord's absolute control over events and people. At the same time, Saul, with all his power and military might, is utterly humiliated. It's his family who save David, and Saul himself ends up, quite literally, publicly taking his clothes off under the Lord's direction (v. 24). David is saved through weakness, and Saul is humiliated into weakness.

Don't be anxious about the seeming weakness of the church in the face of a hostile world. Don't be overwhelmed when you hear stories of persecution. This is the biblical pattern for God's king and his people. We're saved through weakness.

REFLECTION

1. How do you feel about being weak in front of others? How can God use that?

2. What confidence are God's people given here in the face of powerful opponents?

DAY 22

READ 1 Samuel 20:1–42

Commitment is about loyalty and love in the face of discouragement and difficulty. Discipleship is all about a radical commitment to Jesus: 'If anyone comes to me and does not hate his father and mother, his wife and children, his brothers and sisters – yes, even his own life – he cannot be my disciple' (Luke 14:26). We've already seen Jonathan's tremendous risk-taking courage in 1 Samuel 14, but now we see his risk-taking commitment to the true king.

This chapter is all about the commitment Jonathan is willing to make to David in the face of Saul's intentions to kill David. Essentially, Jonathan has to choose which side to be on, and he chooses the kingdom of David rather than the kingdom of his dad, Saul. This commitment is a very deep, costly and profound one. It has the form of a covenant, which, in the Bible, is a binding commitment of love sealed with promises. We see that the language of 'covenant' is used throughout the chapter (see vv. 14–15, 17, 42).

Jonathan makes a covenantal commitment to David in verse 16. In other words, he binds himself to David in the most solemn way possible, and calls the Lord as witness to it (vv. 8, 21, 42). The crown prince, amazingly, has deliberately sided with the Lord's chosen king above his own father (vv. 9, 30), and even above his own future kingdom (vv. 14–15, 31). He has chosen David when David is on the run, hunted down by Saul and everything is against him. Nonetheless, Jonathan, with eyes of big faith, trusts that the Lord will give David the final victory (v. 15).

We're being shown here what commitment to the persecuted king means. It means loving Jesus above family, our own success and prosperity. It's about living out a solemn, binding promise to put his priorities and his kingdom before everything else in our life. Do we have Jonathan's big eyes of faith to see what is coming?

REFLECTION

1. Why is Jesus worth this kind of commitment?

2. Why might that commitment seem costly here and now?

DAY 23

READ 1 Samuel 21:1 – 23:29

Jesus says, to potential followers, 'Foxes have holes and birds of the air have nests, but the Son of Man has nowhere to lay his head' (Matt. 8:20). David is giving us a preview of what this means, as the chosen king becomes a hunted, homeless and persecuted king.

David's life is now a life on the run, hiding in caves and surrounded by enemies. Saul is trying to kill him and David has to flee as best he can. At every point, he looks incredibly vulnerable. In 21:10–15 he has to flee to his old enemies, the Philistines, and only escapes by the skin of his teeth and some skilful deception. Then in 22:3–5 he moves to Moab to live amongst another enemy, but has to flee again. In 22:6–23 we see the kingdom of darkness pursuing David, as Saul slaughters God's priests at Nob. Further, there is always the threat of traitors willing to hand David over – Doeg the Edomite (21:7 and 22:9–10, 18), the city of Keilah (23:12) and the Ziphites (23:19–20). David is besieged by enemies.

Yet, in the middle of this, the Lord sustains his chosen king. David may be homeless and hunted, but the Lord's hand is with him. When desperately hungry, David is given not just any old bread by the priests of Nob, but the living bread of God's presence (21:4–6). He even picks up Goliath's old sword on the way (21:9)! The Lord provides him with a band of loyal followers (21:2 and 22:2), and gives David his word through Gad (22:5) and Abiathar (23:9–12). Finally, the Lord saves David through a number of 'coincidences' – a chance conversation (23:25) and a timely message for Saul (23:26–28).

Following the king isn't an easy, trouble-free life. It can be a life surrounded by enemies. Jesus warned us of this. Yet, the Lord is close and he'll keep us, his homeless, exiled people, going as we seek a better home with him.

REFLECTION

1. How does this passage help you count the cost of following King Jesus?

2. How has the Lord sustained you in the past in the middle of difficulty?

DAY 24

READ 1 Samuel 24:1–22

Jesus says that it isn't the way we treat our friends that defines us, but how we treat our enemies (Matt 5:43–48). David, the Lord's chosen king, has a big enemy – the rejected king, Saul. David has been falsely accused, attacked and hounded from place to place by Saul, but now it seems that the tables have turned. Saul, completely unaware, wanders into the cave where David is hiding out, in order to relieve himself (vv. 1–3). Surely this is the moment David has been waiting for; the Lord has intervened and given Saul into David's hands (v. 4)! David now, miraculously, is in a position of power over his enemy. So, what does he do?

Well, despite constant provocation, and the encouragement of his own men, David refuses to kill Saul (v. 6). Rather, he cuts a corner off the robe (interestingly see also 15:27–28) and then, once Saul is done, presents it to him as proof of his good intentions. David doesn't see an opportunity to take power, but an opportunity to live by faith. He *trusts* that Saul has been given his power by God (vv. 6, 10) and that only the Lord can remove him. David knows that he's innocent (vv. 11, 14–15) and he *trusts* the Lord to judge between him and Saul (vv. 12, 15). He acts in mercy because he is living by *faith* in his God. As a result, Saul is clearly moved by David's actions and speech (vv. 16–21), and even admits David's claim to the throne (v. 20), showing the power of faith as it shows itself in love.

We're told about the Lord Jesus: 'When they hurled their insults at him, he did not retaliate; when he suffered, he made no threats. Instead, he entrusted himself to him who judges justly' (1 Pet. 2:23). We have a meek and merciful king who doesn't seek revenge, and who lets his Father sort out the justice of the situation. We can follow his lead with the challenging situations in our own lives.

REFLECTION

1. What impressed you about David's actions here? How does that point us to Jesus?

2. Where do you need to trust the Lord's justice in your life today?

DAY 25

READ 1 Samuel 25:1–44

Disciples with even a small amount of self-insight know how easily they can be overcome by sin. This is the case too with David, the chosen king. In 1 Samuel 24 we saw David's meekness and mercy, but here in 1 Samuel 25 we see David's violence as he comes to the brink of committing an atrocity!

The days are already dark because Samuel, God's great prophet, has died (v. 1). And David is now provoked by a wealthy, prosperous farmer called Nabal. His name actually means 'fool' in Hebrew! Nabal shows himself to live up to his name (vv. 3, 14, 25). In response to a request for help (vv. 2–9), he insults David and his men (vv. 10–11), provoking David to come and kill him (and others). It's very striking to see here how David's restraint with Saul isn't repeated with Nabal. In fact, David is starting to follow Saul's methods (see 22:6–19). Nabal is undoubtedly a fool, but David is also acting like a fool himself. The passage is warning us that, like David, we too can, in a moment, fall away into sin and foolishness.

Ironically, the only thing that stands between David and an atrocity is a wise woman, Abigail. She takes responsibility in the situation, appeases David's anger (vv. 18–25) and, remarkably, refocuses David on the Lord's sovereign plan and justice (vv. 26–31). Her speech was the speech David had just given Saul outside the cave (see 24:11–15)! David is immediately convicted and recognises the evil of what he was about to commit, as well as Abigail's role in preventing it (vv. 32–34).

Let's be thankful for the countless times the Lord has restrained us from evil, and even sent us our own 'Abigails'. And let's imitate the wise man in Proverbs, who always listens to correction (Prov. 13:18). That may be the only thing that stands between us and a sin we'll come to regret.

REFLECTION

1. Are you being tempted to anything at the moment that is foolish or sinful? How will you resist it?

2. How good are you at listening to the wisdom of others? Do you feel that you need it?

DAY 26

READ 1 Samuel 26:1–25

Chapter 26 echoes chapter 24. The setting to the story is very similar to chapter 24, with, once again, Saul pursuing David to kill him, and David showing restraint as the Lord gives Saul into his hands. We see here that David has grasped something deeply which we all need to grasp: our rise and fall are in the Lord's hands (vv. 9–10). Even while he is on the run, and in a position of weakness, David knows that the Lord is in control of everything.

We see his faith at work in the story, as his actions prove to be even bolder than in chapter 24. Whereas in that chapter Saul happens to wander into the cave where David is hiding, here David deliberately enters the heart of the enemy camp where Saul is (vv. 5 7). Convictions about the Lord's sovereign control (which we see in vv. 8 and 12) give David courage and restraint in attacking Saul (v. 10). In fact, David is, to Saul's humiliation, able to steal Saul's spear. This spear was both a symbol of Saul's power and the very thing that Saul had previously used to try to kill David (18:11; 19:9). The end result is a clear conscience for David (vv. 17–20) and the conviction of Saul's conscience (v. 21).

We should think hard about David's words in verses 23–24. David knows that the Lord is the one who rewards, gives, values and delivers. If we believe that, we'll be able to imitate both the courage and the restraint of David in our own lives. Innocence is one of the first casualties when we're in conflict with people, but it's worth fighting for. We can be courageous today because the Lord is in control of every enemy that threatens us. And yet, in being courageous, we don't need to take the law into our own hands precisely because the Lord is in control.

REFLECTION

1. Give the Lord thanks today for all the ways in which he is in control of your life.

2. Do you need more God-centred restraint at the moment, or more God-centred courage?

DAY 27

READ 1 Samuel 27:1 – 28:2

David has been the hero so far in 1 Samuel, but now the chosen king looks more like Saul. In chapter 25 we saw how David was on the verge of committing great evil (25:33), but here in this chapter we see him actually commit atrocities. This reads, in many ways, as a God-less chapter (the name of the Lord isn't mentioned once). It certainly undermines any temptation to hero worship of David.

David's fall from grace begins in verse 1, with his decision to leave the promised land for Philistia (he did this once before in 21:10–15, but didn't settle there). We may sympathise, but his attitude here is full of fear and not faith (contrast with 26:10, 23–24). He seems to have forgotten the Lord's promises. Accordingly, David moves away from God's people to settle in a pagan nation. This is the city which had previously stolen the ark of the covenant (see chapter 5), and against which he had fought earlier (see chapter 17 – and note also that Goliath was from Gath!). Feeling hurt, mistreated or rejected, individuals sometimes slip into leaving the gathering of God's people, but it's never a good spiritual policy to leave the church behind. God's church is the place where God's blessing has been promised.

David then leads a lifestyle of theft and murder, managing to break a whole number of the ten commandments in one fell swoop (vv. 8–10). He also ends up double-dealing with their king, Achish. While giving the appearance of being a traitor to Israel, he lies to the king about what he's really doing (27:12 - 28:2). This is a clever survival strategy, and it works for David, yet it is God-less and faith-less. David thinks that death is worse than sin, but Jesus shows us that sin is worse than death (Heb. 12:3–4). Our true king gave his life rather than sin (Mark 14:36). Jesus is our model, not David.

REFLECTION

1. Where are you sometimes tempted to think that the end justifies the means? Why is that a faith-less way of thinking?

2. 'Sin is worse than death': why is that? What difference does that make to your decision-making?

DAY 28

READ 1 Samuel 28:3–25

Saul is in dire straits as we begin the chapter, with a huge Philistine army poised to invade. He's overwhelmed with terror (v. 5) and without the Lord's guidance (v. 6). It seems like his kingdom is finally about to fall apart. In sheer desperation, and with utter hypocrisy (see v. 3), Saul goes to a medium to get some guidance as to what to do (see Lev. 19:31, 20:6 where this is forbidden). The medium conjures up the spirit of Samuel from the dead (vv. 8–19).

Of course, we may have many questions about this strange event, but God's purpose here isn't to satisfy our curiosity. Rather the point is to expose the spiritual confusion and sense of being lost that comes from rejecting his word. This story reminds us of how defenceless and desperate we are without the word of the Lord. So, when the spirit of Samuel speaks (and there's nothing in the story to suggest that it isn't, in some mysterious way, the spirit of Samuel), Saul receives exactly the same word that he received earlier in 15:22–29! Effectively, prophet Samuel pronounces one more time that Saul's kingdom is at an end, and that the Lord is about to hand him over to his enemies.

Needless to say, this story isn't a recommendation of spiritism, but simply a depiction of Saul's terrible spiritual feeling of being lost. That disorientation becomes very clear in verses 20–25, where we see an overwhelmed and terrified Saul.

Of course, we may, like Saul, know that turning away from God's word is a bad thing to do. However, this story about Saul's desperate sadness and spiritual confusion serves as a powerful antidote to spiritual hard-heartedness. It reminds us that when we leave God's word behind, there isn't much left to help us. Who wants to end up like Saul?

REFLECTION

1. Praise God for giving you the Bible. Ask him to give you a deep love for it.

2. Is there anyone you know who's in danger of turning away like Saul? How can you help them?

DAY 29

READ 1 Samuel 29:1–11

Sometimes we can get ourselves into complicated and destructive situations through our own bad decisions and wrong-headed thinking. David had himself caught in such a situation in chapter 28, whereby he had been both double-dealing with the Philistines and then, in 28:1–2, somehow got conscripted into their army. So, in chapter 29, David finds himself stuck between a rock and a hard place as he marches with the Philistine army on Israel (vv. 1–2). What hope is there for us when we find ourselves in a mess of our own making?

Amazingly, in the story, the deliverance comes through the intervention of the Philistine top brass (v. 3). They are (rightly) very suspicious of David (vv. 4–5) and don't want him around. King Achish, ironically, tries to defend David against his own military leaders (v. 3), but fails and ends up apologising to David for his being wronged (vv. 6–7)! Surprisingly, David is released, unharmed, from the Philistine army (vv. 10–11), and so escapes the terrible dilemma of being caught between an invading army and his own people. (Notice how no such escape came for Saul in 28:20–25.)

We're meant to see the Lord at work in this. His name isn't explicitly mentioned, and yet often it isn't in such stories (see the book of Esther as an example). Nonetheless, we're meant to conclude that David, the chosen king, has been remarkably rescued by the Lord through his use of pagan military leaders. Isn't it amazing to see how the Lord will sometimes use even our enemies to save us? And isn't it remarkable to see the Lord's mercy to us when we least deserve it? The fact is that the Lord's plan will prevail despite the failings and foolishness of his own people. He can keep us even when we walk off the way. This isn't an excuse for presumption, but a reason for gratitude and wonder at God's work in our lives.

REFLECTION

1. How have you experienced the Lord using 'enemies' in your life to do you good, or even save you in some way?

2. Are you trusting the Lord to keep you and save you for the future, or are you putting your hope in your own wisdom and good decision-making?

DAY 30

READ 1 Samuel 30:1–31

Is Jesus enough for you when you find yourself in a disaster zone? Is he able to work good in your life when everything seems to be falling apart? David's followers here seem to be losing their faith in the king very fast indeed. Ziklag, their home city, has been sacked and plundered (vv. 1, 16), and their wives and children carried off (vv. 2–3). David's band of followers now want someone to blame, and David becomes the object of their anger (v. 6). Can God's chosen king sort this out? Is he up to the task? The answer is: yes!

David can do it because the Lord gives him the strength he needs (v. 6) and guides him with his word (vv. 7–8; see chapter 28 for the contrast with Saul). We've already been told many times in 1 Samuel that the Lord will give David victory wherever he goes (20:15; 25:29; 26:25), and here we see yet another astounding victory from the Lord's hand. With a depleted force (vv. 9–10), David beats what must have been an overwhelming enemy. We're told that 'none of them got away, except four hundred young men' (v. 14). Amazingly, we also learn: 'Nothing was missing ... David brought everything back' (v. 19). It's clear here that we shouldn't let the disasters in our life determine our view of our King's power and might. He's fully able to redeem every single thing from our life. We can trust him.

As David wins yet another great victory, the spoils of war are distributed. The emphasis here is on the king's generosity and grace. *Everyone* is rewarded with the spoils – both those who stayed behind in the battle (vv. 23–24) and others living across the whole land (vv. 27–31). Though some want to limit the rewards to those who have fought (v. 22), David knows that, in reality, everything has come from the Lord (v. 23). Our King, the Lord Jesus, has won a greater battle on the cross. We have no rights to anything, but he loves to lavish good gifts on us. We have a very generous King (Matt. 20:1–16).

REFLECTION

1. What is Jesus able to do for you?

2. How do you see his generosity at work in your life?

READ 1 Samuel 31:1–13

This final chapter in 1 Samuel presents a seemingly hopeless situation for God's people. It brings to culmination something that has already been made very clear: Saul and his kingdom are under God's judgment (15:28; 28:17–19).

The story returns to the battle of Gilboa (see 28:1–4), and picks up the story at the end of chapter 28. The battle becomes an utter disaster for Israel. The royal family is wiped out (v. 2), and Saul ends up having to commit suicide to avoid being taken captive (v. 4). The house of Saul comes to an end in one fell swoop and Israel is invaded, with the people having to flee for their lives (v. 7).

Not only is this a defeat, though; it is a total humiliation. The Philistines mutilate Saul's corpse and take his armour as a war trophy (vv. 8–10). Their message is loud and clear: 'Don't mess with the Philistines – or else!' Of course, there is breathtaking courage in the middle of defeat as the people of Jabesh Gilead (saved by Saul in chapter 11) steal back the king's body (vv. 11 13). But, in reality, this is a desperate end to 1 Samuel. It seems like Israel is over. We're reminded that life in this world can be hard for God's people. There are times when it can seem that the church is beaten and the kingdom of God is at an end.

If we look at this chapter alone, it is depressing. But if we put this chapter into the story of 1–2 Samuel, we can see that the Lord is working out a bigger plan. In the middle of this judgment, we have the good news that the Lord is raising up his anointed one, David, to replace Saul. The kingdom is not at an end! And, if we put 1–2 Samuel into the bigger story of the Bible, then have the hope of the true anointed one, Jesus Christ. One day he will return to bring the fullness of his kingdom. There is hope in the darkness.

REFLECTION

1. How should we respond when it seems that God's people have been defeated?

2. How can we find hope when everything seems dark?

MORE IN THIS SERIES

ROMANS
Momentous News
By David Cook
ISBN: 978-1-906173-24-1

MARK
The Suffering Servant
By Jeremy McQuoid
ISBN: 978-1-906173-55-5

DANIEL
Far From Home
By Justin Mote
ISBN: 978-1-906173-68-5

1 THESSALONIANS
Living for Jesus
By Julia Marsden
ISBN: 978-1-906173-67-8

PHILIPPIANS
Press Towards the Goal
By Kay Mumford
ISBN: 978-1-909611-31-3

GALATIANS
The Life I Now Live
By Peter Mead
ISBN: 978-1-910587-09-6

ACTS
To the Ends of the Earth
By David Cook
ISBN: 978-1-909611-02-3

EZEKIEL
For His Glory
By Peter Lau
ISBN: 978-1-909611-83-2

JOHN
Never Thirst Again
By David Cook
ISBN: 978-1-909611-30-6

and more at... 10 Publishing
a division of 10ofthose.com

To place an order call: **0844 879 3243** email: **sales@10ofthose.com**
or order online: **www.10ofthose.com**